DE LA RUE
STRAW HATS TO SECURITIES

Ian Moncrief-Scott

Information Management Solutions Limited

ISLE OF MAN

The author Ian Moncrief-Scott has asserted his right under the Copyright, Designs and Patents Act 1988 to be identified as the author of this work.

Copyright. © I. Moncrief-Scott 2021

All rights reserved. No part of this publication may be produced in any form or by any means - graphic, electronic, or mechanical, including photocopying, recording, taping, or information storage and retrieval systems - without the prior permission in writing of the publishers.

The publishers make no representation, express or implied, regarding the accuracy of the information contained in this book and cannot accept any legal responsibility for any errors or omissions that may take place.

A CIP catalogue record for this book is available from the British Library.

Published by Information Management Solutions Limited, 17 Howe Road, Onchan, Isle of Man, IM3 2BB.

Printed, bound and distributed by IngramSpark.

Book Layout © 2017 BookDesignTemplates.com

Superhero Peg Image: Besjunior/Shutterstock.com

Cover Source by Tanja Prokop of BookDesignTemplates.com

DE LA RUE: STRAW HATS TO SECURITIES – 2nd ed.
ISBN 9781903467046

The Publishers have been requested by the author to acknowledge the direct and indirect contributions to this book by De La Rue PLC.

This book is dedicated to
start-up entrepreneurs.

The front cover depicts
ordinary wooden clothes pegs dressed as
Super Heroes.

**All start-up entrepreneurs are
ordinary people
turning into Super Heroes!**

CONTENTS

DE LA RUE STRAW HATS TO SECURITIES 1
BIBLIOGRAPHY 13
OTHER BOOKS BY THE AUTHOR 15
FORTHCOMING BOOKS BY THE AUTHOR 17

DE LA RUE
STRAW HATS TO SECURITIES

While other Guernseymen prospered from privateering in the English Channel, fortune did not bless the household De La Rue. Nine children had depleted Eleazer's resources. His son, Thomas, had arrived as Madam Guillotine severed the reign of King Louis XVI.

It was 1793.

After his apprenticeship, the young Thomas tasted printing with the 'Publiciste' newspaper before publishing his own 'Miroir Politique.' But like Dick Wittington, aged 25, he headed for London.

Waterloo had left England in a deep depression. The monarch was mad. Much reform was needed. Uncomfortable with the idea of printing in the competitive capital and high newspaper taxes, Thomas ventured into straw hat making.

Traditionally, beavers provided the substrate for bonnets. America had temporarily offset the shortage that had swept

Europe, but the 1812-14 war cut supplies. Thomas vigorously pursued success. Recounting his printing experience, he experimented with paper bonnets, under a French patent, using waterproofing and colour.

By 1824, embossed bookbinding attracted his attention and he formed a stationery partnership with Samuel Cornish and William Frederick Rock in 1830. As 'Cardmakers, Hot Pressers and Enamellers', they operated from Queen Street, Finsbury.

Bibliomania was sweeping London.

In 1829 Thomas and Mr. Balne of Gracechurch Street published a large royal edition of the New Testament, using gold powder for special copies. Later editions in 1834 and 1836 ensured De La Rue became deluxe.

Thomas was now synonymous with quality!

Meanwhile, Paul, his youngest brother, had joined the firm, now 'Wholesale Dealers in Leghorns, Chops and Straws'. The years 1831 and 1832 were significant for Thomas. De La Rue's first playing card was registered at Somerset House. 'His present most Excellent Majesty King William IV', granted a Royal Letters Patent for 'Certain Improvements in Making or Manufacturing and Ornamenting Playing Cards.'

Until then, cards had been hand-stencilled with watercolours or printed in one colour and hand-tinted. A costly, tedious and inexact process. Imagine trying hand colour fifty-two matched cards.

With innovation in mind, Thomas animated the wooden characters and revolutionised the reverse of the cards. He was soon 'the father of the English playing card and visiting card'.

Some called him the inventor of modern English colour printing, after patenting 'For Improvements in Producing Coloured Steel Plate, Copper Plate and Other Impressions'.

Bunhill Row's notable address appeared in 1834. It housed the new partnership of De La Rue, James and Rudd, 'Cardmakers, Embossers and Wholesale Fancy Stationers'. Thomas enlisted his son Warren, whose scientific paper on the Daniell electric battery led to electro-plating in typography, revolutionising security printing.

Times became difficult for the nation in 1837. On 26 May, long before public limited companies, Thomas was arrested for debt.

His old partnership dissolved, with new associates Fry and Nathan, he resolved to put matters in order. 1838 was make or break. De La Rue's ingenuity, his white lead patent and an £8500 loan from Mr. Charles Button, a wealthy chemist and chemical equipment importer, ensured a positive outcome.

On 28 June 1838, to celebrate Queen Victoria's coronation, he printed the Sun newspaper in gold. It sold out.

His innovation and foresight excelled. In 1840, he registered, 'Improvements in printing calicoes and surfaces'. This invention, using the Jacquard wire loom, enabled tartan-check patterns.

Post Office envelopes arrived in 1839. Previously, writing paper had been folded, sealed and the address written on the reverse. Security was poor.

A year later, Rowland Hill's prepaid Penny Postage scheme, with standard charges and regular deliveries, catapulted the Victorian propensity to correspond. By the decade's end, one million letters a day were being sent.

Aged 23, Warren supervised the 'erection of some large white lead works, the drawings for which he made himself entirely'. He also invented a special boiler, 'so constructed that the fine aroma of the tea was not lost'.

By 1832, The Duke of Wellington had established a railway. Cautiously remarking that this 'enabled the lower classes to travel about needlessly.'

De la Rue won its first order of railway tickets from the London Blackwall Railway in 1841. By 1846 the Company was making tickets for almost all railways in the UK. Within ten years, it was producing 1.5 million per week.

Thomas was introduced to the Tsar of all the Russias Court in 1843. He and Paul were so proficient that within four years, the Tsar's playing cards production multiplied from one to four million packs annually, becoming the world's largest manufacturer.

In St. Peterburg, Paul became friendly with the Winans, from Baltimore, USA, who were building the Trans-Siberian Railway. Eventually, Paul's daughter, Maria Ann, married Walter, son of millionaire Ross Winans. Though living in the

North, he was suspected of potentially delivering his extensive rolling-stock to the Confederacy and was imprisoned twice.

These relationships helped William Frederick obtain the famous Confederate stamp orders from Major Ben F Ficklin. The Five Cent Blue, with Jefferson Davies and the One Cent Orange, bearing John C Calhoun's head, were designed by Joubert de la Ferte.

The initial order was successfully delivered to Wilmington by the blockade runner Robert E Lee. Other consignments created the notorious Mercedita and Bermuda incidents.

However, De La Rue still opened its New York office a decade before the one in Paris.

Partners were being changed back in Bunhill Row. Button, the last outsider, departed in 1844 satisfied that Warren was now established. The firm now specialised in the fancy Victorian stationery, though until 1856, playing cards remained the core business.

After volunteering for the 4th Tower Hamlets, William Frederick became known as 'Colonel Billy'. Warren moved impressively in scientific circles, especially astronomy and lunar photography. His advice was increasingly sought on matters of commerce.

Both he and Thomas were heavily involved in the 1851 Great Exhibition at the Crystal Palace, the 1853 New York and the 1855 Paris Expositions.

April 1853 saw the Board of Inland Revenue move to employ adhesive fiscal stamps on drafts and receipts. De La Rue's improved typographical, or surface printing, vanquished all competition.

The Company started printing stamps for the East India Company. To strengthen its expertise, Dr. Hugo Muller, a Bavarian, was added to the staff. He perfected 'fugitive inks', a vital security feature that prevented cancellation marks from being erased for re-use.

In 1857 Colonel Billy overhauled Bunhill Row. The business had mushroomed and a plan was needed. To coax staff to drink tea instead of beer, Warren and Colonel Billy promoted a Tea Society.

Although the Company had a presence in India, Perkins Bacon, through the Crown Agents, dominated colonial stamps. Despite having only produced a small order for Ceylon, De La Rue capitalised on a mistake by Perkins Bacon. Colonel Billy's close relationship with the new Crown appointee Penrose Julyan clinched all the business.

With no experience of banknotes either, De La Rue was awarded the prestigious Mauritian £5, £1, & 10/- notes, the first of 109 issues made for various countries.

Long term printing contracts flowed. All Indian postage stamps ensued for 71 years, Ceylon 73 years, Great Britain 55 years. Lasting alliances with Italy, Ecuador, Uruguay, and Portugal developed.

Improving all the time, Thomas patented the two-colour process and better watermarking. Between 1857 and 1868, railway ticket output doubled, playing cards reached 265,000 packs.

Sadly, in 1866 aged 74, Thomas died and was buried in the fashionable Kensal Green cemetery.

Tragically, four years later, liver cancer struck 47-year-old Colonel Billy, then also Chairman of Eagle Star Insurance. His passing left the company unsettled.

Warren engaged his sons, Thomas Andros and Warren William. Quality stationery maintained its prestige, the copyright notepaper 'Imperial Treasury' and 'Fine Old Turkey Mill' were hugely popular. Warren's third son, Ernest, contributed ideas for firelighters, pocketbooks and bookmarkers.

In March 1877, the Globe newspaper heavily criticised Perkins Bacon, whose stamp contract was expiring, stating that De La Rue's receipt stamp was far better. The firm's moment to seize superiority had arrived.

Its letterpress technology and international experience won the new Penny Stamp contract.

From November 1879 to June 1881, the company made almost 1.5 billion One Penny stamps alone. Three new printing works were built, the Crown, George and Star. The future was glowing.

Something peculiar happened in April 1897, two years before Warren died. Nigeria complained about De La Rue stamps. Others followed, complaining the gumming was unsatisfactory.

The British Board of the Inland Revenue was emphatic in its support for the Company against Colonial attack. No further complaints were made, such was the pre-eminence.

Young Warren committed suicide. Although now a public company, the family and its friends still owned nearly all the shares. Thomas Andros ruled as a dictator.

Unexpectedly, Uganda rejected new designs, in preference to Waterlow & Sons copperplate-printed examples.

The writing was on the wall.

Thomas Andros's three sons arrived, Evelyn, noted for his 'Onoto' fountain pen invention, Ivor and Stuart. Edwardian days rolled comfortably on. All were blissfully unaware of impending disaster.

During 1911 the Inland Revenue proposed to divide its contract, awarding the higher denominations to De La Rue and the lower (more profitable) ones to Harrisons, which had never printed a stamp. In a fit of arrogant pique, Thomas Andros refused to share the contract. It was lost forever. He died some months later.

The outbreak of the Great War brought a brief respite. HM Treasury fearing a run on gold, gave the company an order for 2.5 million 10/- Treasury Notes. Waterlow Brothers and Layton (WB&L) printed the £1 denomination.

The second edition order was reversed after Stuart made a fuss. De La Rue printed all £1 sharing the 10/- notes with WB&L.

Later in the war, the Government realised that security improvement was needed to prevent forgery. De la Rue and Waterlow & Sons (not WB&L) conspired to defeat competition by a convenient tacit agreement.

To their mutual annoyance, the entire contract went to WB&L because of its new cheaper photogravure process.

With Thomas Andros and Evelyn in the army, Stuart was in sole charge. He was a hapless businessman. While other producers prospered during the war, the company reversed a £90,000 profit into a £90,000 loss.

Though De La Rue was struggling, some key Waterlow & Sons staff joined the company, bringing design, engraving and engineering photogravure expertise. Stuart left the firm after the competition conspiracy scandal emerged, ending the family reign.

Company affairs were again in disorder. Fifty-year-old machinery appeared in the books at full value.

Coincidently, the next day the Siamese Government wrote advising they wanted new currency. Bernard Westall was immediately despatched to prepare a tender.

While awaiting the outcome, he learned that Government was encountering forged customs certificates.

Westall knew Prince Viwat, a Cambridge contemporary, working in the Customs House and convinced him to introduce a De La Rue security device into customs forms.

The five-year banknote order was also secured.

A Spanish Government bond contract quickly followed.

Life was being breathed into the business. Overseas, salesmen Peter Loopuyt and Albert Avramov were appointed.

Acting for the American Banknote Company, the latter had beaten Waterlow & Sons to a Bulgarian order by bribing the Finance Minister. While Avramov escaped on the Simplon Express, the Minister was not so lucky. He was hanged for corruption.

Between Loopuyt and Avarmov, extensive banknote and stamp contracts flowed, including four billion postage stamps for China. Even the playing cards improved. 1932 provided a timely centenary for Thomas's 1832 patent for 'Improvements to Playing Cards'.

To emphasise the Company's metamorphosis and ensure foreign Finance Ministers never again doubted its stability, Westall launched the famous Annual Dinners. These were a resounding success and the guest list read like the United Nations Assembly.

Substantial Chinese business was secured. At £3 million, the largest order in the Company's history was snatched from ABC's grasp. De La Rue was back and would surge into the world's largest securities producer.

Having swallowed rivals Bradbury Wilkinson, Waterlow & Sons, Harrison and papermakers Portals, today De La Rue manufactures most facets of the money business.

From ATMs, coins, credit cards, smartcards, and passports to software, holograms, cheques, stamps, banknotes, and bonds worldwide.

Not a bad achievement for a straw hat maker from Guernsey.

BIBLIOGRAPHY

Houseman, L. (1968). The House That Thomas Built. London: Chatto & Windus.

OTHER BOOKS BY THE AUTHOR

As Good As Gold - History of Pound Sterling. ISBN 0-9534818-4-0

Currants, Olives & Cotton (eBook). ISBN 9781903467169

De La Rue Straw Hats to Global Securities. ISBN 0- 9534818-2-4
De La Rue (eBook). 9781903467138

Euro History & Development. ISBN 0-9534818-1-6

Holidays 2000 – A Time Capsule. ISBN 0-9534818-7-5

Negotiate to Win! - The Introductory Edition. ISBN 0-9534818-6-7

Start Any Business (Print). ISBN 9781903467008
Start Any Business (eBook). ISBN 9781903467015

Scripophily - Historic Bond & Share Collecting. ISBN 0-9534818-5-9

The Eternal Old Lady - Bank of England. ISBN 0-9534818-3-2

The Green Shoots of Money (Print). ISBN 9781903467107
The Green Shoots of Money (eBook). ISBN 9781903467114

The Hitmen - Part One. ISBN 0-9534818-8-3

FORTHCOMING BOOKS BY THE AUTHOR

As Good As Gold (Print). ISBN 9781903467039
As Good As Gold (eBook). ISBN 9781903467121

Currants, Olives & Cotton (Print). ISBN 9781903467077
Currants, Olives & Cotton (eBook). ISBN 9781903467169

Euro (Print). ISBN 9781903467053
Euro (eBook). ISBN 9781903467145

Scripophily (Print). ISBN 9781903467084
Scripophily (eBook). ISBN 9781903467176

Tail-less Cats & Three-legged Men (Print). ISBN 9781903467091
Tail-less Cats & Three-legged Men (eBook). ISBN 9781903467183

The Eternal Old Lady (Print). ISBN 9781903467060
The Eternal Old Lady (eBook). ISBN 9781903467152

ABOUT THE AUTHOR

Ian Moncrief-Scott has over fifty years of broad business experience, mostly gained at international level, based in the UK.

As a former senior executive for a global publishing and information technology company headquartered in the USA, he has contributed to numerous client-facing procurement and outsourcing initiatives worldwide.

Ian has created and participated in numerous small businesses in the UK, Isle of Man and elsewhere.

He has also represented the Isle of Man Government Department for Enterprise in several of its business support schemes. Ian designed and delivered extensive training for its Micro Business Grant Scheme.

In recognition of his long-term service to the Department, Ian was nominated for The Queen's Award for Enterprise Promotion and awarded an official Certificate of Recognition in 2018.

Throughout his career, he has maintained an active interest in start-ups, especially those involving the financial sector.

At the turn of the millennium, several of the articles written by Ian that form this short work were originally published by the Museum of American Financial History (now the Museum of American Finance).

www.ingramcontent.com/pod-product-compliance
Lightning Source LLC
Chambersburg PA
CBHW071551080526
44588CB00011B/1867